KEVIN DURANT

NBA STAR

By Douglas Lynne

Book design by Jake Nordby
Cover design by Jake Nordby

Photographs ©: Melissa Tamez/Icon Sportswire/AP Images, cover, 1; Carlos Avila Gonzalez/San Francisco Chronicle/AP Images, 4, 23; Tony Dejak/AP Images, 6–7, 9, 18; Sue Ogrocki/AP Images, 10; Joe Don Buckner/AP Images, 13; John Froschauer/AP Images, 14–15; Ted S. Warren/AP Images, 16; Ashley Landis/AP Images, 20; Red Line Editorial, 22

Press Box Books, an imprint of Press Room Editions.

Library of Congress Control Number: 2023909036

ISBN
978-1-63494-756-5 (library bound)
978-1-63494-763-3 (paperback)
978-1-63494-776-3 (epub)
978-1-63494-770-1 (hosted ebook)

Distributed by North Star Editions, Inc.
2297 Waters Drive
Mendota Heights, MN 55120
www.northstareditions.com

Printed in the United States of America
102023

ABOUT THE AUTHOR

Douglas Lynne is a freelance writer. He spent many years working in the media, first in newspapers and later for online organizations, covering everything from breaking news to politics to entertainment to sports. He lives in Minneapolis, Minnesota.

TABLE OF CONTENTS

CHAPTER 1
Big-Time Player 4

CHAPTER 2
Second Best 10

CHAPTER 3
One of a Kind 16

Timeline Map 22
At-a-Glance 23
More Information 23
Glossary 24
Index 24

GOLDEN STATE
35
WARRIORS

1

BIG-TIME PLAYER

The Golden State Warriors needed a spark. They trailed the Cleveland Cavaliers 113–109 in Game 3 of the 2017 National Basketball Association (NBA) Finals. Less than 2:00 remained in the game, and Cleveland had the ball. That's when Kevin Durant stepped up.

Cavaliers star LeBron James missed a shot, and Durant grabbed the rebound. Then Durant dribbled the length of the

Durant is as tall as a center, but he dribbles like a guard.

Durant plays defense against Cleveland superstar LeBron James.

court, breezing past defenders. However, the Cavaliers fouled him on his way to the basket.

Durant got the ball on the inbound pass. Dribbling outside the three-point line, he

waited for his moment. He drove to his left and powered his way toward the rim. But then he stopped short, fooling his defender. Durant drained an easy jump shot, hitting nothing but net. The Warriors still trailed by two with only 1:15 to go.

After Cleveland missed a shot, Durant pulled down another rebound. This time, he calmly jogged up the court. As Durant reached the three-point line, his defender took a step back. Durant released a perfect shot. The ball swished through the net. Durant's three-pointer gave the Warriors a 114–113 lead with 45 seconds left.

SUPER TEAM

The win in Game 3 gave Golden State a 15–0 record in the 2017 playoffs. The Warriors lost Game 4 but won Game 5 to claim the championship. Durant helped lead the Warriors to a 16–1 playoff record. That was the best in NBA history.

The Cavaliers tried desperately to score, but they couldn't connect. Golden State held on to win 118–113. In fact, the Warriors scored the final 11 points of the game. Seven of those points came from Durant. He was at his best when his team needed him most.

Durant drives to the basket to score two of his team-high 31 points in Game 3.

TEXAS
35
MONDS

2

SECOND BEST

Kevin Durant was born on September 29, 1988, in Washington, DC. His mother, Wanda, raised Kevin and his siblings on her own for most of Kevin's early life. Kevin was a natural at basketball. He stood 6 feet tall by the time he reached middle school.

When Kevin was 13, his father, Wayne Pratt, came back into his life. Pratt cheered for Kevin at his basketball games. Kevin

Durant dunks over a defender during a college game.

played with many talented players. Some of them would end up in the NBA.

By his senior year of high school, Kevin had grown to 6-foot-7. He was tall enough to be a center. But he had spent years learning to play like a guard. His size, combined with his ability to dribble and shoot, made him tough to defend.

Experts ranked Kevin as the second-best high school player in the country. Many top colleges wanted him to play basketball for them. Kevin chose the University of Texas.

Durant didn't like being ranked second. He wanted to be the best. As a 6-foot-9 freshman

A SPECIAL NUMBER

Durant has worn the number 35 for most of his career. He chose that number for a reason. One of his favorite coaches, Charles Craig, died at age 35. Durant has worn that number to honor Coach Craig.

When Durant had the basketball, he was always a threat to pass or shoot.

at Texas, he became one of the top players in the country. He averaged more than 25 points and 11 rebounds per game. At the end of the season, Durant won the John R. Wooden Award. This trophy is given to each season's best college basketball player.

Durant and his new teammate Jeff Green show off their jerseys after joining the Seattle SuperSonics.

After just one year in college in 2006–07, Durant was ready to turn pro. He decided to enter the 2007 NBA Draft. Durant felt he was the best player and should be picked first.

However, he came in second again. Greg Oden was chosen ahead of him. The Seattle SuperSonics drafted Durant with the second overall pick. That gave Durant the drive to keep improving.

SONICS
35
SEATTLE
SONICS
22

3

ONE OF A KIND

Kevin Durant was still a teenager when he entered the NBA. His opponents were older and stronger. Yet Durant quickly became an NBA star. In his first season with Seattle, he averaged more than 20 points per game. He won the 2008 NBA Rookie of the Year Award.

The following season, the SuperSonics moved. They became the Oklahoma City Thunder. Durant changed too. He grew

Durant spent one year with the SuperSonics before the team moved to Oklahoma City.

Durant's tall body and long arms give him an advantage against smaller players.

to 6-foot-10, the height of a center. But he kept practicing the skills of a guard. He became even better at dribbling and shooting. And it showed. In his third season, Durant led the NBA in scoring. At age 21, he was the youngest player ever to do so. Durant also led the league in scoring for each of the next two seasons.

In 2012, he helped Oklahoma City reach the NBA Finals. However, Durant and the Thunder lost to the Miami Heat.

In the years that followed, Durant was nearly impossible to stop. Other teams didn't know how to defend him. He was too fast for other big men. But he was too tall for other guards. After the 2013–14 season, Durant won the NBA Most Valuable Player (MVP) Award.

By the end of the 2015–16 season, Durant was ready for a change. He left Oklahoma City and signed with the Golden State Warriors. Durant helped his new team win NBA titles in 2017 and 2018. Both times, Durant earned the Finals MVP.

THE REAL MVP

Kevin Durant held back tears as he was awarded the 2014 NBA MVP. He thanked his mother, Wanda, for her support. He also said that she was the real MVP.

Durant reaches out and steals the ball from his opponent.

In 2019, Durant wanted a new challenge. He left the Warriors and signed with the Brooklyn Nets. Unfortunately, an injury forced him to sit out a full season. By the end of 2020, he was back on the court. Even with Durant, Brooklyn never reached the Finals. Durant asked the Nets to trade him. In early 2023, the Nets sent him to the Phoenix Suns.

By this point, Durant didn't have anything left to prove. Fans agreed that he was one of the greatest scorers in NBA history.

KEVIN DURANT

CAREER STATISTICS (PER GAME)

- **2007–08** – 20.3 points, 4.4 rebounds, 2.4 assists
- **2008–09** – 25.3 points, 6.5 rebounds, 2.8 assists
- **2009–10** – 30.1 points, 7.6 rebounds, 2.8 assists
- **2010–11** – 27.7 points, 6.8 rebounds, 2.7 assists
- **2011–12** – 28.0 points, 8.0 rebounds, 3.5 assists
- **2012–13** – 28.1 points, 7.9 rebounds, 4.6 assists
- **2013–14** – 32.0 points, 7.4 rebounds, 5.5 assists
- **2014–15** – 25.4 points, 6.6 rebounds, 4.1 assists
- **2015–16** – 28.2 points, 8.2 rebounds, 5.0 assists
- **2016–17** – 25.1 points, 8.3 rebounds, 4.8 assists
- **2017–18** – 26.4 points, 6.8 rebounds, 5.4 assists
- **2018–19** – 26.0 points, 6.4 rebounds, 5.9 assists
- **2019–20** – did not play
- **2020–21** – 26.9 points, 7.1 rebounds, 5.6 assists
- **2021–22** – 29.9 points, 7.4 rebounds, 6.4 assists
- **2022–23** – 29.1 points, 6.7 rebounds, 5.0 assists

TIMELINE MAP

1. **Washington, DC: 1988**
   Kevin Durant is born on September 29.
2. **Rockville, Maryland: 2006**
   Durant grows to 6-foot-7 and finishes his high school career at Montrose Christian School.
3. **Austin, Texas: 2007**
   Durant completes his only year in college at the University of Texas. He earns the John R. Wooden Award as the best college player.
4. **New York, New York: 2007**
   Durant is selected second overall by the Seattle SuperSonics in the NBA Draft.
5. **Oklahoma City, Oklahoma: 2012**
   Durant leads the NBA in scoring for the third straight season. He also plays in his first NBA Finals.
6. **Oakland, California: 2017**
   Durant wins his first NBA title, helping the Golden State Warriors beat the Cleveland Cavaliers.
7. **Brooklyn, New York: 2019**
   Durant joins the Brooklyn Nets after three years with the Warriors.
8. **Phoenix, Arizona: 2023**
   Durant is traded to the Phoenix Suns in a deal that includes players from four different teams.

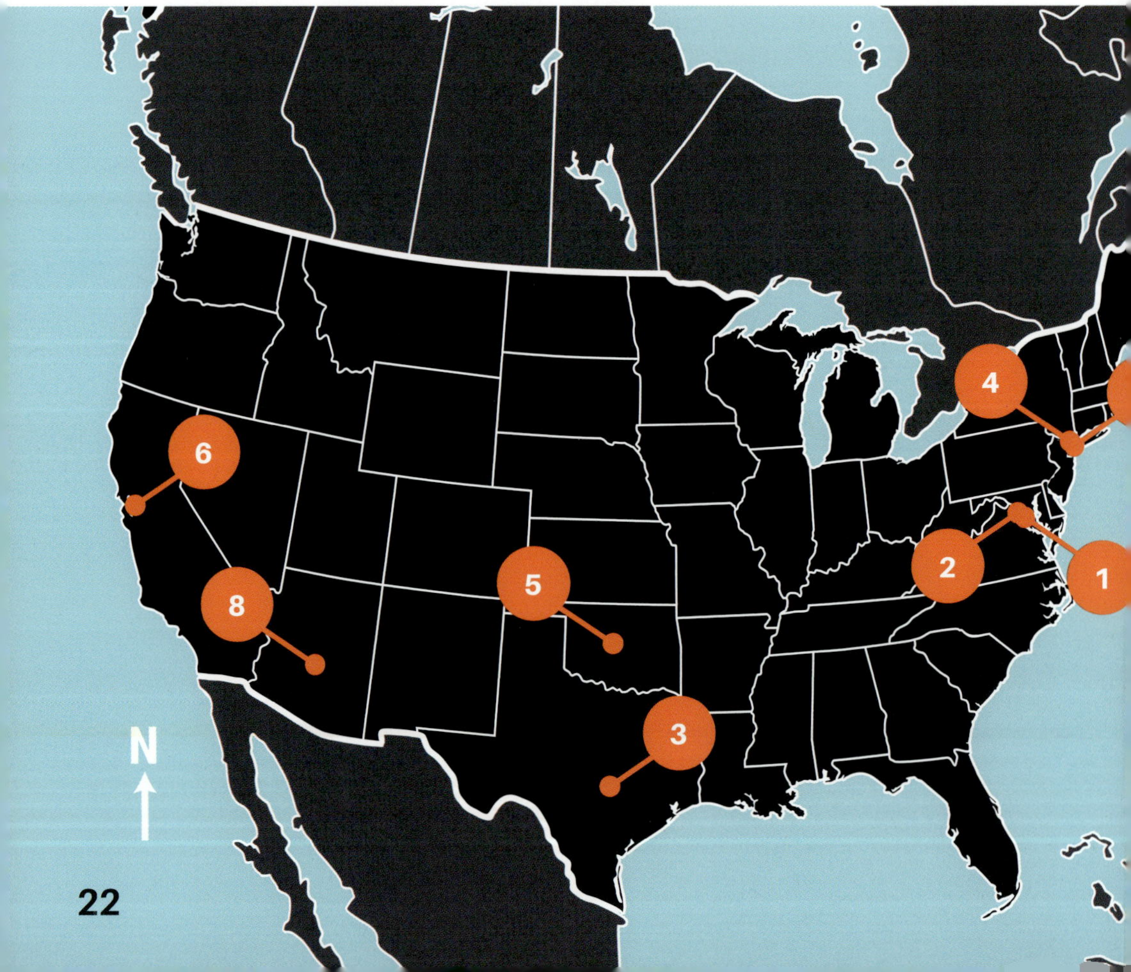

AT-A-GLANCE

KEVIN DURANT

Birth date: September 29, 1988

Birthplace: Washington, DC

Position: Forward

Height: 6 feet 10 inches

Weight: 240 pounds

Current team: Phoenix Suns (2023-)

Past teams: Texas Longhorns (2006-07), Seattle SuperSonics/Oklahoma City Thunder (2007-16) Golden State Warriors (2016-19), Brooklyn Nets (2019-23)

Major awards: NBA Rookie of the Year (2008), First-Team All-NBA (2010-14, 2018), NBA All-Star (2010-19, 2021-23), NBA All-Star Game MVP (2012, 2019), NBA MVP (2014), NBA Finals MVP (2017, 2018), NBA Champion (2017, 2018), NBA Scoring Champion (2010-12, 2014)

Accurate through the 2022-23 season.

MORE INFORMATION

To learn more about Kevin Durant, go to **pressboxbooks.com/AllAccess**.

These links are routinely monitored and updated to provide the most current information available.

GLOSSARY

draft
An event that allows teams to choose new players coming into the league.

Finals
In the NBA, a series in which the first team to win four games is champion.

inbound pass
A pass from out-of-bounds that begins play after a foul, timeout, or turnover.

natural
A person born with a skill or special ability to do something.

swished
Made a basket that went through the net without touching the rim.

trade
To exchange players or draft picks with another team.

INDEX

Brooklyn Nets, 20

Cleveland Cavaliers, 5–8
Craig, Charles, 12

Durant, Wanda, 11, 19

Golden State Warriors, 5–8, 19–20

James, LeBron, 5
John R. Wooden Award, 13

Miami Heat, 19

NBA Draft, 14–15
NBA Finals, 5–8, 19–20

Oden, Greg, 15
Oklahoma City Thunder, 17–19

Phoenix Suns, 20
Pratt, Wayne, 11

Seattle SuperSonics, 15, 17

University of Texas, 12–13